An Eagle Flies High

Written by Alice Pernick

W9-BEI-111

There is a nest in the highest tree.

The nest looks like a big pile of sticks.

The nest is the home of an eagle.

The eagle is a large bird.

1   2   3

1   2   3

Its wings can open seven feet wide.

This eagle's head, neck, and tail are white.

The rest of it is brown.

An eagle can see very well.

It can see things that are far away.

An eagle likes to eat fish.

That's why an eagle lives close to a river or sea.

But an eagle can't swim.

It uses its beak and legs to catch fish.

An eagle feeds the fish to its babies.

A baby eagle is called an eaglet.

An eaglet stays in the nest for many weeks.

The eaglet grows up and leaves the nest in the tree.

A new eagle flies high.

A new eagle flies free.